Scotch Malt Whisky Investment & Enjoyment 2015

DR. MICHAEL J. ROSS

Copyright © 2015 Dr. Michael J. Ross

All rights reserved.

DEDICATION

To Anna, my editor, wife and dramming companion.

CONTENTS

1	Introduction	1
2	What is whisky?	5
3	The whisky regions	10
4	What to buy	13
5	Where to buy and sell	26
6	Building the knowledge	34
7	More than just a dram	38
8	What next for whisky?	43
9	How to hold a whisky tasting	47
10	Whisky tasting note sheet	51

1 INTRODUCTION

Haggis. Square sausage. Irn bru. Red Kola. Deep fried pizza. Deep fried Mars bars. Culinary delights Scotland gave the world and every Scotsman is supposed to love and be proud of. Except we don't. Most people I know do not care much for these things.

But there is one thing that we get passionate about. Whisky. Strangely it is blended whisky that makes up 90% of all sales. But it is malt that we love and cherish, that we order on a cold winter night in front of the fire, that we spin the glass to see the treacley legs, to savour its smooth vanilla burn, or cough on its choking peatiness as it claws at our throat. There's nothing quite like it. And if you are reading these words then you agree.

My first taste of whisky was the classic Bells blend, made into a 'hot toddie' to treat my cold, or perhaps just to get me off to sleep so I didn't interrupt my Nana's night in with her old friend Mrs Dow, drinking Bells and Crabbie's green ginger. In my mid-teens I remember my friend, Ian, and I helping ourselves to his parents Drambuie, after they had headed out at Hogmanay to 'first foot' their neighbours.

In my late teens I was drinking Jack Daniels, the spirit of choice for the rock scene. I was then introduced to Laphroaig, the well-known peaty medicine, by friends, Some years passed before my love of whisky was rekindled by the wonderful Caol Ila, a much under-rated Islay, at a cousin's wedding in Aberfoyle, where I drank so much of it that the barman gave me the bottle. I had just met my sweet wife, Anna, and was high on the joys of life.

A couple of years later I happened across a fascinating TV documentary about the re-opening of the Bruichladdich distillery by a few whisky lovers. Bruichladdich were looking for people to put their money into 'Futures', whisky to buy now and collect later. This seemed like a great wedding present for my wife to give me, so I duly persuaded her. Not more than a year later I got made redundant, and I quickly realised that I needed to find something to invest my redundancy payment in, or else I would likely spent it all on beer in the pub. So started my journey into the world of whisky investment.

While waiting for my cask to mature, I started buying two bottles of whisky at a time, intending to have one to drink, and one to sell on in order to cover the cost of the one drunk. I had a particular passion for quirky Murray McDavid bottlings, such as the *Leapfrog* and the *Springbank Cuvee*, and set about collecting all I could find around the world.

However I soon had too many bottles open in the house, and I realised that some whiskies were simply too high in value to start opening at a whim. I wanted to know more about whisky, so I completed the Whisky Course Certificate of the University of the Highlands and Islands Moray College/ Gordon & MacPhail, and became a member of the Scotch Malt Whisky Society. Like many people I started taking an interest in whisky history, and the closed distilleries, the bottles of which are highly collected e.g. the *Diageo Rare Malts Selection*.

Whilst boring my friends incessantly talking about whisky in the pub, other people I met showed great interest in knowing more about the investment side of whisky. I realised that although there were many books about whisky, there were none I could find about investment. And so I decided to write this guide to help people who were interested in it to get off to a good start.

This guide covers:

1. This introduction;
2. What is whisky? – how flavour is created, and the importance of age and the cask on price;
3. The whisky regions – and what they mean for taste, and ownership;
4. What to buy – the different reason a bottle can have investment value, and pitfalls to avoid;
5. Where to buy and sell – how to locate whisky, recommended international suppliers, and places to sell;
6. Building the knowledge – recommended books, festivals, distillery maps, websites and blogs;
7. More than just a dram – how whisky is expanding its use in food, drink, and by women;
8. What next for whisky – where the investment market is going;
9. How to hold a whisky tasting
10. Tasting note sheet.

Before we go further I should explain that I do not consider myself a whisky tasting expert. There are simply too many whiskies and I have a responsible day job. I'll never be Jim Murray, Charles MacLean, Dominic Roskrow, ... the list goes on. I've also met some real unsung experts, such as the barman at the Dornoch Hotel, the staff at Boisdale in London, the ladies at the Bow Bar in Edinburgh.

But I do realise that I have some good experiences to share that should help you get more out of malt whisky, and hopefully help it pay for itself.

"Today's rain is tomorrow's whisky"

2 WHAT IS WHISKY?

The term whisky comes from the Gaelic 'uisge beatha', or 'usquebaugh', meaning 'water of life'. Quite simply, whisky is a beer made from fermented barley, which is then distilled to give a strong spirit. It is a complex process of mash tuns, worts and other such jargon, but you don't really need to know that. If you want to know more, a good guide is at Maltmadness.com[1].

After 3 years storage in wood casks it can be called whisky. Prior to bottling it may be cooled and filtered (chill-filtered), to stop it going cloudy at low temperatures. It may also have caramel added to give it a deeper colour. It can then either be bottled neat, lightly diluted, or diluted to a minimum of 40% alcohol by volume (80° proof), a strength that doesn't burn your tongue.

The whisky varieties
The 5 types of Scotch whisky recognised by the Scotch Whisky Association are:

---

[1] www.maltmadness.com/malt-whisky/beginners-guide-to-scotch.html

1. single malt - made from malted barley at one distillery;
2. single grain - made from grain other than barley at one distillery;
3. blended malt (also called vatted malt) - from more than 1 distillery;
4. blended grain - from more than 1 distillery;
5. blended - a mix of malt and grain. It's hard to believe, but blended whisky has only really been widely available since the 1960s.

Most large distilleries tend to mix a number of different casks to give a consistent flavour, perhaps 15 to 50. These can be different ages, so the official age of a whisky as on the bottle is taken as the age of the youngest whisky in the mix. Age is calculated as the time in the cask, generally between distilling and bottling. Older whiskies are generally more expensive, for reasons explained later.

The creation of flavour

It is important to understand how whisky gets its flavour, the four main influences being:

1. Whether or not the barley is germinated using peat as the heating fuel (the 'malting' process);
2. The shape of the distillation apparatus. Taller stills tend to produce lighter, purer, whiskies;
3. The number of times distilled. Three times is the normal, and more times distilled means lighter, purer, whisky;
4. The cask used for storage before bottling. Basically any cask can be used. The cask may or may not have already been used to age whisky (i.e. first fill or refill). Whiskies may be put into more than one type of cask to give it an extra flavour 'finish'.

The most common casks are bourbon and sherry,

simply because they traditionally used to be cheap second-hand leftovers from the US bourbon and Spanish sherry industry. We canny Scots know how to save money. But if you can name a wine cask, it has probably been tried, even champagne, though it's fair to say some work better than others. I still have a barely touched bottle of *Arran Grand Cru Champagne Finish* in my house, which I once bought hoping it would be a hit with the ladies coming to a party. Unfortunately it was massive disappointment, with too much wood flavour rather than champagne.

The importance of the cask

The most collectable (and investable) whiskies tend to be single malt, and 'single cask', bottled from one cask. It's therefore important to bear in mind that there are different sizes of cask, which affects how many bottles can be produced.

- *Quarter, Octave cask*: 50 litres; 11 UK gallons; 13 US gallons;
- *Bourbon cask*: 200 litres; 44 UK gallons; 53 US gallons;
- *Hogshead cask*: 250 litres; 55 UK gallons; 66 US gallons;
- *Sherry Butt, Port Puncheon cask*: 500 litres; 110 UK gallons; 132 US gallons;
- *Port Pipe cask*: 650 litres; 143 UK gallons; 172 US gallons;
- *Tun cask*: 1000 litres; 220 UK gallons; 264 US gallons.

Most Scottish distilleries now import casks whole, although Balvenie still have their own 'cooper', to rebuild the imported wooden parts of casks (staves).

The amount of whisky bottled is always less than the original put in the cask due to the "Angels share" (or more accurately, "Devil's share"). The loss rate is often quoted at around 2% each year, but can be up to 10%, due to four main reasons:

- the original strength of the spirit;
- the atmosphere in the storage area, with lower losses in cool damp locations with less temperature fluctuations (unlike the USA where bourbon evaporation rates are very high);
- how well the cask has been made, how often and how carefully it is moved around;
- and of course theft - Balvenie tell the story of the warehouseman that went into his jacket pocket to get his favourite 'dipping dog' (a pipe on a rope[2]), only to find it had been found, flattened, and replaced in the pocket as a warning message.

These losses are the reason why older whiskies are more expensive, because there will be less volume to bottle and sell as time goes by. The minimum % for sale in the UK is 40%, so this means that each whisky has limited time it can spend in the cask, and whiskies in cask are regularly tested to determine the right time for bottling. In 2008 Diageo experimented with wrapping their cask with cling film, in an effort to reduce the losses. However, it is also argued that as whisky gets some of its flavour from oxidation, less air will mean less flavour. Only time will tell.

Older is not always better. Taste comes from the other alcohol previously in the cask, but then it starts to leach resins and oils from the wood cask. This is why bourbon has a vanilla flavour. Like wine, fifty year olds are prized but rarely drunk.

It is debatable whether or not single cask tastes better than single malt or blend. Single cask aficionados will argue that a blend is always a good whisky with less good

---

[2] uk.thebalvenie.com/news/the-dipping-dog

whisky, so the overall result is a less good whisky. Others will argue that blending adds extra taste, and mellows out any imperfections, whereas a single cask can be 'corked' like wine.

One thing is certain – mixing whiskies can bring fantastic new flavours. For instance, I recently enjoyed the *Douglas Laing Caol Ila & Tamdhu Double Barrel*. Compass Box have based their entire business on the concept of blends. The *Murray McDavid Springbank Cuvee* blended malt attracted a lot of interest when it was released, as a blend of a little 38 year old with a lot of 10 year old Springbank. Recently the *Balvenie Tun 1401* batch releases have been well received, with resale prices rising to over 5 times the original price. And people are willing to pay for 'super deluxe' blends like *Johnnie Walker*. So don't be a whisky snob, give all whiskies a try and make up your own mind what you like.

"It doesn't matter how good your English is, as long as your Scotch is good"

3 THE WHISKY REGIONS

The Scotch Whisky Association recognises five whisky regions in Scotland, although collectors and sellers tend to use six:

Historic split	Scotch Whisky Association old split	Scotch Whisky Association current split	Collectors / sellers split	Common Characteristics of taste
Highland	Highland (inc Campbeltown)	Highland	Highland	Varied, often robust
Lowland	Lowland	Lowland	Lowland	Light, floral/grassy
Islay	Islay	Islay	Islay	Peaty, smoky, medicinal
Campbeltown		Campbeltown	Campbeltown	Dry, heavy, rich
	Speyside	Speyside	Speyside	Sweet, fruity, sherried
			Islands	Soft, salty, light peat

The regions are now a somewhat outdated concept but still used. Originally they existed to make it easier to regulate and license the distilleries. Some of you will have realised that Speyside, Campbeltown and Islay are part of the Highlands, and Islay is of course an island. More recently we have added a new Island, with the Abhainn Dearg distillery on the Isle of Lewis in the Hebrides, and there are plans afoot to set up a distillery in the Shetland Isles.

There has also been great change in the numbers of distilleries operating. In 1777, there were only 8 legal distilleries (but many illegal) due the tax on whisky. By 1895[3] this had risen to 140, only to sharply reduce to around 40 in 1933.[4] Currently there are 107 working distilleries and another 8 in planning.[5]

Islay's whisky heritage as the birthplace of whisky in Scotland has always been of such importance that it deserves its own region, and its whiskies are highly prized by collectors. At one point it was estimated that there were up to 23 distilleries in Islay, now reduced to 9. Similarly the Lowlands hardly merits being a region of its own these days, with many lamented silent distilleries, but big changes are afoot, as I discuss in later chapters.

In recent times whisky drinkers have found it easier to split the regions by taste of the whisky. However, that is also changing. Distillers are looking for ways to attract new customers, or steal them from other distilleries, and new distilleries are popping up. For instance, for whiskies whose taste does not follow the regional patterns, try *Laphroaig Triple Wood*, *Kilchoman Sherry Cask*, *Benromach Peat Smoke*, or *Balvenie Islay Cask* (and its peated cask replacement).

Who owns the distilleries?

The sadder thing is that although we Scots are fiercely proud of our whisky, very little of it is owned by Scots now.[6] In addition about 90% of our whisky is exported.

---

[3] The Distillery Map of Scotland, Chas. Mackinlay & Co., 1895.
[4] Scotch Missed: Scotland's Lost Distilleries, Brian Townsend, The Angel's Share, 2000 (reprint Neil Wilson Publishing Ltd., 2004).
[5] List of whisky distilleries in Scotland, Wikipedia,
en.wikipedia.org/wiki/List_of_whisky_distilleries_in_Scotland#Malt_whisky_distilleries

Good for our economy, but bad for our cupboards. International names like Louis Vuitton Moet Hennessey, Pernod Ricard, and Bacardi are well known for other drinks. Japanese whisky companies Suntory and Nikka are building knowledge and expertise to take home to their main distilleries. And by far the biggest name is the mega-brand Diageo. But there are still some names in Scottish ownership such as Glenfiddich, Balvenie, Macallan, Highland Park, Springbank, as well as smaller such as Kilchoman and Abhainn Dearg. Sadly Bruichladdich was sold on to Remy Cointreau recently, but leaves behind the legacy of creating the world's peatiest whiskies with the *Octomore* range.

> *"Water in my Scotch? I'm thirsty, not dirty!"*

---

[6] See www.whisky-emporium.com/UK/Features/WhoOwnsWhat.htm, www.maltmadness.com/whisky/index.html and the Malt Whisky Yearbook 2014, p199.

4 WHAT TO BUY

There are 3 main reasons to buy whisky:
- to drink;
- to collect – which I consider a form of investing; and
- to invest.

In the past year or so I've enjoyed drinking and would recommend for beginners the *Aberlour Abunadh*, *Balvenie Doublewood*, and *Dalmore Cigar Malt*. However these are not the sort of whiskies I would invest in. The following provides a few pointers on how people decide what to collect and invest in.

What to buy and why

First editions - The first bottle in any series tends to be the one that is hardest to get hold of as time goes by, and collectors will pay a huge premium to complete their collection. If sold initially at a normal price it's quite common for them to be drunk rather than collected, reducing the number on the market. Some examples include the *Balvenie Tun 1401*, *Bruichladdich DNA*, and *Flora and Fauna* white sealed bottlings.

Closed (silent) distilleries - When a distillery shuts, there will only be so much whisky left in stock, and of course stock is not being replenished. It's worth remembering that some silent distilleries are more silent than other. Companies looking to recover their investment quickly have flooded the market with low age whisky as soon as they could. The more commercially astute owners have drip fed whisky onto the market in small batches, keeping demand and prices high, whilst retaining some stock for later releases. And of course some older drinkers have a sentimental attachment to their favourite whiskies of old, so are willing to pay more to track down the last bottles in circulation.

Distillery only - Many distilleries offer a 'distillery only' bottling as an incentive to get people to come and visit them. But not everyone will have the opportunity to come to Scotland, or travel to the most remote distilleries. The bottlings are also usually changed annually. So these bottling are rarer and more highly prized, though prices vary. For example, while I was happy to drink the *Talisker* bottle I picked up on a visit to Skye, I parted company with a *Macallan Easter Elchies*. Resale prices for the latter are now running to several hundred GBP.

Festival bottlings - Bottlings produced for a particular festival are collectable, and often a place to pilot or road test something more unusual. Lagavulin have been sponsoring a jazz festival from several years, also releasing a festival bottling to coincide. Kilchoman have been very active in producing bottling for various festivals around the world e.g. the Dramfest in New Zealand. However, by far the most celebrated bottling are those for the Feis Ile, the week-long festival of music and malt on Islay in May each year. Some of these bottles are hard earned, with people having to get to Islay, then queue in the rain at the distillery to get their hands on one, but it can be well worth it. For example, the *Port Ellen 2008 Feis Ile* bottling is now changing hands for around 2,000 GBP (3,330 USD). A few decent purchases and that's your festival holiday paid for.

Press packs - Some malts are released as miniatures that never get sold separately in shops, and/or are sent to various members of the Press or known tasters. Recent examples of minis that have generated high auction prices include *Ardbeg Day*, *Ardbeg Alligator*, and *Macallan Easter Elchies*.

Limited releases - This is a subjective term of course. Small distilleries may release only 200-500 bottles, whereas larger ones may run to several thousands. A good rule of thumb is that the release will likely be collectable if it runs to 2000 bottles or less, and bottles are individually numbered.

Collections - As with the 'first editions', collectors will pay a huge premium to complete their collection, and it's likely that prices will continue to rise as these become more scarce. For instance, there are a number of bottling in *Diageo Rare Malt Selection* range, most of which sells for around 200 GBP (330 USD) but the Brora is now exchanging for over 2,000 GBP (3,330 USD) due to its rarity. Other well-known collections include *Flora and Fauna*, *Bowmore Black/White/Gold Trilogy*, *Arran Icons*, *Glenmorangie Wood Finish*, *Glendronach Single Cask*, and *Diageo Annual Releases*. More recently launched collections have seen prices rise sharply, such as the *Bruichladdich Octomore* series, *Highland Park Earl Magnus* and *Valhalla* collections, and bottles from *That Boutique-y Whisky Company*.

Old whisky - It's generally held that older whisky is better tasting, and certainly the prices are higher. In some ways this is justifiable given it has to spend more time unsold, and being cared for while in the cask, not to mention the losses due to the 'angel's share'. However, I have found that it is not true in all cases. I was fairly disappointed with a bottle of *Speymalt 50 year old* I once bought, being a bit too woody rather than nicely sherried.

Most of the big distilleries have a nondescript 30 year old bottling, but there are some much more special whiskies that attract attention. For instance, about 4 years ago you could get an *Ardbeg Lord of the Isles 25 year old* for around 250 GBP (415 USD). Now, you can expect to pay double that. Other decent old whiskies with good returns are *Glenmorangie Oloroso cask 30 year old*, and *Lagavulin 30 year old*.

Older whiskies are still making it onto the market at affordable prices, such as the *Diageo Annual Release 2013 Talisker 35 year old*, and the *Douglas Laing Old Particular* series which included a *Port Ellen 31 year* old at about 320 GBP (530 USD), half the price of the same whisky as a 33 year old *Diageo Annual Release*. Master of Malt recently released a 60 year old malt for 1000 GBP (1665 USD), which is a fraction of the price of other bottlings of that age.

There has also been a lot of interest in the 'super old' whiskies, which are largely out of the budget of the average collector. For example, the *Gordon & MacPhail Generations* whiskies include *Glenlivet* and *Mortlach* 70 year olds, at a cool 15,000 GBP (25,000 USD) per bottle from some sellers. A slice of the exclusivity can be had by buying a 3cl miniature for around 700 GBP (1,165 USD). Alternatively you could plump for the older *Gordon & Macphail Private Collection* bottlings, where you can still track down bottles around 500 GBP (830 USD). But if you are a millionaire with more money than sense, then the *Dalmore Trinitas 64 year old* for 100,000 GBP (166,500 USD) might be just the bottle for you.

It's also worth noting that the 'magic numbers' of 30, 40, and 50 year old are popular, and easily resold, as these are often bought as birthday or anniversary presents. However, not all old whiskies are collectable. For instance older *Glen Grant* and *Glenfarclas* original bottling are widely available, and not of much interest to collectors at present, but they are tasty for drinking.

Old bottles - Not to be confused with old whisky. Whisky ages in the cask, but not in the bottle. However, some collectors are very keen to get their hands on bottles from bygone eras, even if they are young 10 or 12 year olds. Of particular interest are bottles measured in fluid ounces, with older style labels, or in 'dumpy' bottles (such as those by Cadenhead in the past).

Cask strength - In general, the most collectable whiskies are cask strength, as collectors tend to think that these at the original cask strength and not watered down. However, in practice companies may manipulate the strength a little to ensure consistency. This does not detract from their value, and if you wish to drink these whiskies, then it is worth remembering that you get around 25-50% more alcohol than a standard 40% (80 proof) bottle. Flavour will be stronger if less dilute, but the alcohol could overpower your taste buds. It's a matter of preference of course.

OB not independents - The term OB means 'own bottling' by a distillery, rather than by another independent company. In general OB bottling are more expensive and collectable than independents, and the difference can be quite dramatic e.g. as with the *Douglas Laing Old Particular Port Ellen* described above. Some collectable independents include Gordon and Macphail, Murray McDavid, Moon

Import, Samaroli, Duncan Taylor, Douglas Laing & Co, Wm Cadenhead, Signatory Vintage. For drinking, I would recommend Berry Bros & Rudd, Adelphi Distillery Ltd, Blackadder International Ltd, Dewar Rattray, and the Scotch Malt Whisky Society. See a good list of worldwide independents at www.worldwhisky.org/top/rated-independent-bottlers/.

High scorers - Similar to Robert Parker's wine scoring system, there are also a few very well-known whisky reviewers who's scoring can make or break the desirability of a whisky. Jim's Murray's award[7] of 2010 best malt of the year to *Octomore Orpheus* drove its price to more than triple its original. Serge Valentin's scoring also heavily affects the market.[8]

Heritage - One thing that is common to any market is the appeal of items from our past. Recently two bottles of whisky from the famous SS Politician shipwreck, popularized by the film 'Whisky Galore', went to auction. In 1987 the bottles were sold for 500 GBP (830 USD) each. In 2013 they sold for 6000 GBP (10,000 USD) each. Last year also saw the release of a 'recreation', *Mackinlay's Rare Old Highland Malt*. The recipe is based on analysis of old bottles discovered some 100 years after being abandoned in Antartica during an expedition of explorer Ernest Shackleton, and it is very easy sweet drinking. However, as this release is not so limited, time will tell whether it can appreciate. The experience of the *Macallan 1876* replica would suggest it can, with prices now running to 150-200% of the original launch value.

Celebrity endorsed - again the whisky marketers have managed to add value through tie ins. Macallan have been particularly active with this concept. Their *Private Eye*

---

[7] www.whiskybible.com/
[8] www.whiskyfun.com/

magazine edition is extremely sought after, closely followed by their more recent *Masters of Photography* series featuring stars such as Rankin and Leibovitz.

Gift packs - Wooden boxes tend to make a whisky more collectable, greatly affecting the price of some *Flora and Fauna* editions for instance. However, wood boxes not a reliable indicator of desirability, as even some cheaper whiskies now come in them. It's very common to find bottles with extras such as glasses and hip flasks. However the more collectable bottles tend to have something more unusual. For instance, *Macallan Ghillie's Dram* includes some fishing flies, and its price can now vary anywhere between 150 and 400 GBP (230 and 665 USD). The *Ardbeg Double Barrel* is an extreme example at the other end of the scale, with two bottles in a leather case, with fountain pen, a leather-bound notebook and eight sterling silver cups, coming in at around 10,000 GBP (16,650 USD).

Decanters - these special editions in are surprisingly collectable despite being a somewhat old-fashioned concept. *Dalmore* and *Macallan* appear to be battling it out to see which brand can produce the most expensive bottling. *Macallan M Imperiale* holds the record with 382k GBP (628k USD), upgrading on its *Macallan Lalique* at 300k GBP (460k USD), with *Dalmore Trinitas* close behind at 196k GBP (160k USD). *Gordon & Macphail Generations* releases, *Bowmore 40*, and *Glengoyne*, have been recent decanter editions at more accessible prices, but still beyond the average collector's pocket.

Foreign editions - some launches are only within particular countries or continents. With glass bottles being fragile, couriers refusing to insure, and some customs barring import or export, the availability of these bottles can be very poor internationally, which drives up the price.

For example, the 2012 *Glenfiddich Cask of Dreams* US-only release sells for 150-200% of its purchase price. *Balvenie Tun 1401* editions are similarly in demand.

Superbrands - the more widely a whisky is marketed, the more likely it is known and collected. It's no surprise that whiskies with long term international reach and multi-million dollar marketing budgets have a strong following, such as *Glenlivet*, *Macallan*, *Ardbeg* etc.

'In fashion' - it is worth remembering that there a quite a few whisky speculators out there, and the market price depends on their behavior, in much the same way that the stock markets operate. Collectors and investors don't usually buy for taste, so fashion drives the price to a degree, and people can get caught up in the hype. For instance, will people really want to pay 150 GBP (250 USD) for a 12 year old whisky, when they have a good think about it? Speculators bought into *Glenfiddich Snow Phoenix* in droves, an unusual 'emergency' bottling of whisky following the collapse of a warehouse. From sale at 60 GBP (100 USD), the high of around 160 GBP (266 USD) dropped to 100 GBP (166 USD) due to oversupply, but has showed signs of recovering.

Club releases - with so many whiskies available, whisky companies are keen to try and keep customers loyal. A bone offered from time to time is early or exclusive access to limited releases. Some of the most prized amongst collectors are those from Ardbeg Committee, Springbank Committee, Kilchoman Club, and the Friends of Laphroaig. Some sellers are also very active in getting editions badged for their own shop e.g. La Maison du Whisky, The Whisky Club, Whisky Galore etc. Joining these clubs is relatively easy and free just by signing up online.

Premiumised - the final trend to watch out is for when distilleries try to reinvent themselves, releasing 'luxury' bottlings aimed at the more affluent buyer, or simply at higher cost. Diageo's tripling of the release price of their Port Ellen has led to a knock on arise in the price of other Port Ellen bottlings. They have released Mortlachs at 180 GBP (300 USD) for an 18 year old, and 600 GBP (995 USD) for a 25 year old, and this is expected to lead to knock on effect on other Mortlach prices.

How to Research

Gone are the days when you had to get hold of auction sales results booklets. These days your best friend is the internet, with most shops and auction houses posting online. See Chapter 5 for more information. However, it's worth bearing in mind that English is not the first language in many countries. Google Translate is a fantastic tool to help you search, ask questions, and read answers from suppliers abroad, and of course there are other programmes that do a similar job.

When to buy

I have found that the three best times to buy are:

1. immediately on release, where high demand is expected;
2. when you can see large price differences for the same bottle in different stores; and
3. when bottles start to run out, as demand starts to outstrip supply.

All of these indicate that there could be a profit to be made. Some stores watch the market price like hawks, but bargains can still be had where sellers are slow to raise their prices.

What to Pay

The first important rule is to realise that for bottling that have been around a while, retail price is not the same as the market price. Shops have overheads to pay, and are happy to keep prices high in an effort to find that one desperate 'big fish' willing to be scalped to get their hands on a rare bottle. A good rule of thumb is to expect to pay/get around two thirds of the average retail price.

You can find a lot of comparative data by looking at auction outputs e.g. McTears in Scotland provides an Excel spreadsheet. One of the best sources is Andy Simpson[9], (aka the Whisky Investor) who provides information on Facebook, Twitter, and for the W Club (The Whisky Shop), and his own site WhiskyHighland.com. Another useful data site is WorldWhiskyIndex.com operating out of the Netherlands.

A second rule of thumb is to consider whether the price has 'peaked'. General 'drinking whisky' prices are up to 150 GBP (250 USD) for a 10 year old, up to 200 GBP (333 USD) for a 20 year old, and up to 400 GBP (666 USD) for a 30 year old. Unless there is something particularly special about the bottling, be cautious about spending more than this in the expectation of a return. A good example is *Ben Wyvis*, a rare whisky with only three editions readily available at present, but where the price has reached a ceiling and not altered significantly over the past 6 years. So aim to buy low, sell high.

A third rule of thumb is to split the risk if you are unsure. Club together with others to buy more expensive bottles, so that you get a second or third opinion on

---

[9] www.facebook.com/pages/The-Whisky-Investor/201781239865704,
www.thewclub.co.uk/auction-watch-with-andy-simpson-part-18/,
www.thewclub.co.uk/tag/whisky-investment/,
www.whiskyhighland.co.uk/discover/whisky_investing.html

whether it's a sensible buy or not. It also keeps the individual cost down if you decide to drink instead of selling on.

Good buys
As you might expect, there are some good and bad whisky buys, and I have had both.

The general school of thought is that casks are not a good investment. They cost money to store and bottle. You cannot predict how much you will lose to the Angel's Share. They are also surprisingly hard to resell, with only a few specialists dealing, and at low prices. Unless you have money to spend on high quality marketing, you are very unlikely to get good resale prices on your own bottles. Plus you have taxes to pay to the Government.

One way you can get a return is to put your money into whisky futures, whereby you are investing now to get your hands on distillery labeled bottles at some point in the future. *Bruichladdich Octomore Futures The Beast* regularly sells for double its original cost. Unfortunately few distilleries are offering futures at present, but it is an area to watch. At the time of writing new cask and bottle offers were available at Strathearn, Isle of Harris Distillers, and Annandale.

One area I would steer any investor away from is the 'curios' market, and by that I mean bottlings you find personally interesting and unusual rather than those clearly valued by the market. At one point I started collecting the Invergordon distillers *Malts of Scotland* series, but soon realised that I was the only one interested in collecting bottles that borrowed the names of the old long-closed distilleries *Ferintosh*, *Kincaple*, *Glenluig*, *Craignure*, and *Druichan*.

Strangely, I did once have in my hands, their related *Ben Wyvis* imposter edition, as a gift I auctioned to raise money for various charities. Glasgow's McTears auction house were quick to point out that it had merely borrowed the name and would not be worth much at auction. I think I sold it for around 50 GBP (83 USD), and regret not buying it myself as a talking point. This was also the first whisky I ever sold.

The reproduction idea has recently been resurrected with *The Lost Distillery Company Stratheden, Auchnagie,* and *Gerston*, attempting to re-create the flavours rather than just borrow the label. And I have already mentioned *Mackinlay's Rare Old Highland Malt.*

I also have old and new shaped bottles of *Muckle Flugga*, and interesting whisky which was intended to be the first whisky distilled on the Shetland Isles, but was actually only ever stored on Shetland. The original bottles mostly went missing, having being stolen from a warehouse, and the project abandoned as the company entered liquidation. The project is now being resurrected by the Shetland Distillery Company, so perhaps some good times are ahead. Similarly, I have a bottle of *Tyndrum Gold*, a special bottling celebrating my small purchase of shares in Scotland's only gold mine, a project which has currently stalled. A true dream dram in the end.

So where have the best buys been of late? Had you bought any of the following over the last few years you would have seen some very good and quick appreciation:

- Ardbeg Lord of the Isles, Kildalton 2014, other Committee bottlings e.g. Perpetuum
- Macallan Coronation, Diamond Jubilee, Royal Marriage, Easter Elchies
- Lagavulin 30

- Laphroaig 30, older aged Cairdeas
- Bruichladdich Octomore Futures The Beast, Orpheus, DNA, PC, Blacker + Redder Still, Black Art
- Glenfiddich Cask of Dreams, Snow Phoenix
- Glenmorangie Oloroso Cask
- Balvenie Tun 1401 early batches, Craftman's Reserve (No1 The Cooper), Rose
- Kilchoman first bottling, Port Cask, Club Sherry Cask
- Diageo Port Ellen and Brora Annual Releases
- Diageo Rare Malt Selection Glenlochy, Brora
- Bowmore Black, White, Devil's Cask
- Arran Peacock, Devil's Punchbowl
- Flora and Fauna collection
- Glendronach bottlings
- Feis Ile bottlings from the Islay Festival of Music and Malt, where not on general release also
- Highland Park Valhalla collection

"Whisky gets better with age. The older I get, the more I like it."

5 WHERE TO BUY AND SELL

There are many distribution channels for buying whisky, but for investing the following are listed in order of best returns:

Distilleries – Go to distilleries if you can, and pick up their distillery only bottling. I know of one commercial seller that travels around Scotland at least once a year in order to get his hands on these rarities.

Shops that don't sell online, or list all their whisky - These often have rarities hiding on the back shelves. For example, I very recently on my travels found Robertsons of Pitlochry, which still had an *Ardbeg Provenance*, *Macallan Royal Marriage*, and *Celtic Heartlands* bottlings on their shelf. I still regret not buying them.

You, family or friends travelling – Whether it's for holiday or work, keep an eye out on travel retail specials as you pass through airport off duty shops, and pop into local whisky specialists. Good returns can be had if you buy abroad what has sold out in your own country. Ask friends and family to pop into the shops on your behalf, or have a bottle delivered to their hotel to make it easier for them. You don't need to be too concerned about having a bottle delivered while they are actually staying, as most hotels will happily store a package for a guest well in advance of their actual stay, as long as they have booked. Of course its good etiquette to give your 'agent' a little thank you present, so bear that extra cost in mind if you are only in this for the money.

People you know abroad – If you are lucky enough to have friends and family living around the world, get them involved. My sister-in-law in Washington was very helpful when I was looking for a *Glenfiddich Cask of Dreams*. Otherwise it is fairly easy to build a network of like-minded contacts, who either sell or swap bottles. Just by sending an email to the websites of an enthusiast in Austria, I managed to get my hands on the Scotch Malt Whisky Society's first *Glenfarclas* bottling, a beautifully sherried malt that I had at one of their special tastings. Whisky lovers of the world unite.

Online – The only problems with online sales is that everyone else sees the same 'shop window', and in recent years I have noticed that it has become harder and harder to find true bargains. If you are willing to buy from abroad, you can still take advantage of currency rate differences, but you will have to factor in paying postage, and possibly paying import taxes. But the internet does offer some benefits. For example, you can get a 10% discount on sales from The Whisky Shop if you pay a small fee to join their W Club. And getting on store mailing lists, Facebook, Blogs or Twitter sites means you get the first notice of good investment bottles coming out for sale.

Below I set out some trusted search sites and stores I can recommend. You can also find many more in the *Malt Whisky Yearbook*, an annual publication.

Search engines
- Google Shopping
- WineSearcher www.Wine-searcher.com USA, searches worldwide. Pro version 43 USD per annum.
- Whisky Finder www.Whiskyfinder.eu Sweden, searches EU

Auctions
- Whisky Auction (EU) www.whiskyauction.com Germany, covers EU
- Whisky Auction (UK) www.whiskyauction.co.uk Scotland (UK)
- Scotch Whisky Auctions www.scotchwhiskyauctions.com Scotland (UK)
- Ebay www.ebay.de, www.ebay.fr, www.ebay.nl Germany, France, Netherlands
- McTears www.mctears.co.uk Scotland (UK)
- Bonhams www.bonhams.com Scotland (UK)
- Mulberry Bank Auctions www.mulberrybankauctions.com Scotland (UK)

Scotland (UK)
- The Whisky Shop Dufftown www.whiskyshopdufftown.co.uk
- Scotch Whisky Experience www.scotchwhiskyexperience.co.uk
- Royal Mile Whisky www.royalmilewhiskies.com
- The Whisky Shop www.whiskyshop.com
- The Green Welly Stop www.thegreenwellystop.co.uk
- Drambusters www.drambusters.com
- Loch Fyne Whisky www.lfw.co.uk
- The Whisky Barrel www.thewhiskybarrel.com

England (UK)
- Nickolls and Perks www.nickollsandperks.co.uk
- Soho Whisky / The Vintage House www.sohowhisky.com

- Arkwrights www.whiskyandwines.com
- Jeroboams www.jeroboams.co.uk
- Drinksupermarket www.drinksupermarket.com
- Amathus www.amathusdrinks.com
- Shop4whisky www.shop4whisky.com
- Wright Wine and Whisky Company www.wineandwhisky.co.uk
- Amps Fine Wines www.ampsfinewines.co.uk
- Eton Vintners www.etonvintners.com
- Gauntleys Fine Wines www.gauntleys.com
- Edencroft Fine Wines www.edencroft.co.uk
- The Whisky Lounge Ltd www.thewhiskylounge.com

Europe
- Lavinia - www.lavinia.fr, www.lavinia.es - Spain, France
- La Maison du Whisky - www.whisky.fr , www.whisky.sg - France, Singapore
- Wijnwinkel Slijterij Ton Overmars - www.tonovermars.nl - Netherlands
- Whiskysite.nl - www.whiskysite.nl - Netherlands
- Banneke - www.banneke.com - Germany
- Finlays Whisky Shop - www.finlayswhiskyshop.de - Germany (and ebay)
- Killis – www.killlis.at - Austria
- Garrafeira Nacional - www.garrafeiranacional.com - Portugal
- Lion's Fine and Rare Whisky www.lionswhisky.com - Italy
- Almada Vini www.almada-vini.com - Italy
- Macandrews Whisky Store (ebay) http://stores.ebay.co.uk/Macandrews-Whisky-Store/Whisky-/_i.html?_fsub=2878819011 - Italy
- Old Whisky http://oldwhisky.net/ - Italy

Other
- Pearson's Wine & Spirits - www.pearsonswine.com - USA (Washington)
- Rare428 - www.rare428.co.jp - Japan
- Whisky Galore - www.whiskygalore.co.nz - New Zealand

Oddly, there are three UK sites that are missing out on the whisky boom. The only sellers that seem to use Amazon in the UK are *Hard to Find Whisky*, who have a good collection, but very high prices, so are not to be recommended unless you are desperate. Gumtree just don't allow alcohol sales. Similarly Ebay UK (who own Gumtree) have stopped allowing whisky sales, because they got caught selling alcohol to underage kids in the US. However this is a poor excuse, as they seem to have no such problem allowing selling on European Ebay sites.

The risks

Unfortunately buying globally is not without risks. For instance, I once bought *Port Ellen* from www.Divinovin.com in France. I was delighted when 2 boxes were delivered to my house, but less delighted to find them empty apart from some tissue. It appeared that either the bottles had not been sent, or that they had been stolen in transit by some postal service staff. The truth would never be clear.

They strung me along for months saying they were investigating, before eventually just stopping corresponding with me. In the end it seemed clear that they were not adequately insured to be able to make the refund, but I was fortunate enough to be able to recover the costs through my credit card company. Another company, www.Hi-spirits.com, tried to sell posters of the whisky instead of the whisky.

It is also very common for firms to have 'attractor' whiskies on sites that ran our years ago. They simply advertise them to get people to come to their sites. Very annoying when you go to the trouble of registering and buying, then hearing that the order can't be fulfilled. Bear in mind that bogus fraudulent sites will use similar tactics to try and get you to come to them and give them your credit card details, so do your homework.

Quite often you will hear about fakes. Surprisingly these still manage to find their way into auction houses, but tend to get spotted by potential buyers. It's not always so easy when you buy direct without a second opinion. Fakers seems to aim for maximum reward, faking high value bottles such as *Macallan*, and a significant number appear to come out of Italy. A good source of advice is Whiskyfun.com.[10]

There are also other practices that go on where the sellers are either naïve or sneaky depending on your point of view. One site would not fulfill my full order, saying that the bottles had run out. That same day I noted that they had relisted the bottles, but doubled the price. Very underhand. Another sent me a bottle where the seal was not properly in place, casting doubts on its authenticity. One seller even sent me the bottles without the boxes, having thrown them in the bin.

So before you buy, check that:

- the photo of the whisky is the actual whisky for sale;
- it is available in the quantity and price you want;
- it has its box; and
- the postage is not just tracked, but adequately insured.

---

[10] www.whiskyfun.com/war.html

It sounds obvious, but let's face it, it's a lot more difficult to get problems sorted out when the firm is on the other side of the world, and does not speak your language. Firms can exploit this, so do your research before buying.

If you want others to take the risk of choosing the whisky to invest in, then you could consider trying the *Whisky Trading Company*[11], *Whisky Investments*[12], *or The Whisky Corporation.*[13] Or if you have a minimum 250k USD to invest, the very new *Platinum Whisky Investment Fund.*[14] But where's the fun in that?

When to sell

I have found that the best two times to sell are immediately after a bottle comes on the market, and when stock runs low/out, perhaps around two years after release. It's a good idea to keep an eye on the market as prices can shift quickly. A nice anecdote is the story of the man who bought the two last known bottles of a certain whisky at auction, went into a pub, and opened one to offer the customers there a drink. One customer asked him why he would do this. The man replied that the remaining bottle left was now priceless, as the last in existence.

Where to sell

Naturally the best profit is to be made selling the whisky direct by yourself. These days it's not too hard to get a free webpage where you can post some photos, and take payment by Paypal, cheque or bank transfer.

In addition to the auctioneers mentioned in the table above, there are some newer ones on the market that

---

[11] www.whiskytradingco.com
[12] www.whiskyinvestments.nl
[13] www.thewhiskycorporation.com
[14] www.theasset.com/article/26215.html#axzz2x0npqDX9

specialise in whisky. Time will tell whether there is enough business for these to survive - www.whisky-onlineauctions.com, www.auctionwhisky.com, www.whiskymarketplace.com, and www.just-whisky.co.uk.

"Sometimes I drink my whisky neat. And sometimes I take my tie off."

6 BUILDING THE KNOWLEDGE

Naturally there are plenty of books, tastings, festivals and blogs for whisky enthusiasts. Some of the best are listed below.

Whisky tasting books
- 101 Whiskies to Try Before You Die (Ian Buxton)
- 1001 whiskies you must taste before you die (Dominic Roskrow)
- Handbook of Whisky: A Complete Guide to the World's Best Malts, Blends and Brands (Dave Broom)
- Malt Whisky Yearbook (various writers- Michael Jackson, Jim Murray, David Wishart, Charles Maclean, Helen Arthur, Ian Wisniewski, Dave Broom, Martine Nouet, Bob Minnekeer, Hans Offringa)
- The Malt Whisky Companion (Michael Jackson)
- The Malt Whisky File (John Lamond & Robin Tucek)
- The Whisky Bible (Jim Murray, annually)
- The Whisky Encyclopedia (Michael Jackson)
- The World's Best Whiskies (Dominic Roskrow)

- Whisky: Malt Whiskies of Scotland - Collins Little Books (Dominic Roskrow)
- Whisky Classified (David Wishart)
- The World Atlas of Whisky (Dave Broom)

Whisky history books
- Malt Whisky: A Liquid History - Charles Maclean
- Scotch Missed: Scotland's Lost Distilleries (Brian Townsend)
- Scotland and its Whiskies (Michael Jackson)
- The Whisky Distilleries of the United Kingdom (Alfred Barnard)
- Whisky & Whiskey (Jim Murray)

Whisky whimsy
- Appreciating Whisky (Phillip Hills)
- How to Blend Scotch Whisky (Alfred Barnard)
- Peat, Smoke & Spirit: A Portrait of Islay and Its Whiskies (Andrew Jefford)
- The Making of Scotch Whisky (Moss & Hume)
- The Whisky Treasury (Walter Schorbert)
- Whiskey Women: The Untold Story of How Women Saved Bourbon, Scotch, and Irish Whiskey (Fred Minnick)
- Whisky Tales (Charles MacLean)

Old whisky distillery maps
- Scotch Whisky Distillery Map 1960.[15]
- Whisky Map of Scotland, Chas Mackinlay & Co, 1895.
- Whisky Map of Scotland, Chas Mackinlay & Co, 1902.[16]

---

[15] www.leap-gallery.com/gallery.html?page=shop.browse&category_id=6
[16] blogs.nls.uk/bartholomew/?p=41

Whisky festivals
- Islay Festival of Music and Malt (Feis Ile)
- The Whisky Fringe Edinburgh
- Edinburgh Whisky Stramash
- Drambusters Festival (Dumfries)
- Aberdeen, Birmingham, York, Chester, Leeds, Newcastle, London, Inverness, Midlands (Stourbridge), Spirit of Stirling, Spirit of Speyside, and Glasgow Whisky Festivals
- TWE Whisky Show (London)
- WhiskyFest New York, Chicago and San Francisco (USA)
- Victoria, Edmonton, and Spirit of Toronto Whisky Festivals (Canada)
- Maltstock, Spirit of Amsterdam, and the International Whisky Festival (Netherlands)
- Stockholm Beer and Whisky Festival (Sweden)
- UISGE Whisky Festival (Finland)
- Oslo Whisky Festival (Norway)
- Tokyo Bottler's Festival (Japan)
- WhiskyLive – a travelling show, in 2014 visiting New York, Moscow, Tel-Aviv (Israel), Australia.

Blogs to read (web/twitter)
- Whiskyadvocate;
- Whiskymag;
- Malt maniacs;
- Dramming.com;
- Whiskymag;
- Whiskyintelligence;
- Linkedin group Whisky-Investment-6583988.

And don't forget to go see The Angel's Share movie for a fun look at the investment pitfalls.

"Whoever said laughter is the best medicine has never had Laphroaig"

7 MORE THAN JUST A DRAM

There is a whisky for everyone, and I am always happy to take up the challenge to prove it.

A man's drink?
Firstly I want to break through the myth that whisky is a man's game. The media latch on to female whisky drinkers as if they are some sort of novelty. Think Scarlett Johansson, Christina Hendricks, Mila Kunis, Kate Moss, Zoe Ball, and Scotland's very own KT Tunstall. It's just the 'Mad Men' effect? The statistics show a different picture, with women estimated[17] to make up 29% of UK whisky drinkers, 25% of worldwide whisky drinkers, and 15% of Scotch Malt Whisky Society members.

Whisky companies are of course very happy with this trend, and actively trying to develop the market further. But the best advocates are of course women who are passionate about whisky, such as

---

[17] Diageo 2013. www.telegraph.co.uk/women/womens-life/10372412/Why-is-whisky-still-a-mans-drink.html , http://www.ft.com/cms/s/0/5317d1f4-58ff-11e3-a7cb-00144feabdc0.html#axzz2u6LemGVD

- Johanne McInnis, aka "whiskylassie"[18]
- Alwynne Gwilt, journalist, aka "misswhisky"[19]
- Femke Tijtsma Sijtsma, aka "whiskygirl"[20]
- Rachel McNeill, tour guide from Islay[21]
- Amy Seton, aka "TheWhiskyMiss", co-founder of the Birmingham Whisky Club[22]
- Allison Patel, aka "whiskywoman" owner of *Brenne* whisky company[23]
- Geraldine Murphy, chair of the Glasgow womens' whisky club, The Pot Still Whisky Girls[24]
- Heather Green, brand ambassador for *Glenfiddich*[25]
- Kate Massey, aka "thewhiskydame", brand ambassador for William Grant & Sons[26]
- Joy Elliott, brand ambassador for Macallan[27]

and the unsung "whiskywomen".[28] Recently the book Whiskey Women: The Untold Story of How Women Saved Bourbon, Scotch, and Irish Whiskey[29] has promoted the profile of women and whisky further. And there are many other women working in lead roles the industry.[30]

Womens' place in the whisky investment world is firmly cemented by the *Glenfiddich Janet Sheed Roberts Reserve*, a 55 year old whisky bottling in celebration of the 110th birthday of the grand-daughter of distillery founder

---

[18] whiskylassie.blogspot.co.uk/
[19] misswhisky.com
[20] whiskygirl.nl/
[21] Whiskyforgirls.com
[22] twitter.com/TheWhiskyMiss
[23] thewhiskywoman.wordpress.com/
[24] www.facebook.com/ThePotStillsWhiskyGirls
[25] twitter.com/HeatherMGreene
[26] thewhiskeydame.com/
[27] twitter.com/thejoyofwhisky
[28] www.thewhiskeywomen.com,
[29] Whiskey Women: The Untold Story of How Women Saved Bourbon, Scotch, and Irish Whiskey Fred Minnick, Potomac Books Inc., 15/10/13.
[30] See The Malt Whisky Yearbooks for a selection of interviews.

William Grant, the oldest woman in Scotland at the time. Who says whisky is bad for you? The 9th of 11 bottles sold for an amazing 94,000 USD (56,476 GBP), at the time the most expensive whisky ever sold. The first bottle can now be found on commercial sale for £123,734 GBP (206,000 USD), having been bought for £46,850 (78,000 USD) in December 2011. Not a bad profit if it sells.

Weaning onto whisky

I'm now regretting introducing my wife to whisky, as naturally she likes all my best (i.e. rarest) whiskies. If you know people that 'don't like whisky', the best way to change their minds is to use it as an ingredient. You can buy whisky flavoured items that often don't have real whisky in them, so be careful that you are getting the real deal.

Meatilicious

If you feel adventurous, then you can pick up *Grants* Whisky Haggis, a whisky flavoured version of our national dish, haggis, in a tin. It keeps well, is available in airports, and passes most countries customs arrangements. It's great for holding a Burns Supper, in celebration of our national poet.[31] However, it's probably not the best thing to engage newcomers to whisky served by itself. So make Chicken Balmoral instead. Slice a chicken breast sliced open, stuff with some haggis, cook in the oven, and serve with mashed potatoes and green beans, topped with a cream sauce made with a dash of whisky. Delicious.

Sweet treats

Scots have a very sweet tooth, probably because we are always carb loading to survive the cold winters. A treat to recommend is Walkers *Glenfiddich* Whisky Cake, which you

---

[31] 25th January annually. Recipe: Haggis on plate. Knife into haggis. Poem on table. Whisky into you. www.visitscotland.com/about/robert-burns/supper-whats-involved

can pick up readily around the world from quality food stores or airport shops.

The most famous Scottish whisky dessert is Cranachan, which is surprisingly easy to make, much like Eton Mess. It's a delicious mix of whipped cream, raspberries, honey, whisky, and toasted pinhead oatmeal and there are several recipe variations available.[32]

Cocktails

One of the best ways to make whisky more accessible to those that 'don't do whisky' is through cocktails. There has been a good push in this area in the past few years and many recipes are available online.[33] Some mixologists have been experimenting with malt spirit 'new make' that has not been casked long enough to be called whisky. Although colourless, malt spirit is generally seen as too fierce to drink neat. *Bruichladdich X4* is a good example to try if you are brave enough.

The most popular whisky cocktails use bourbon, but I want to share a few recipes with you, which are variations using Scottish malt whisky.

Rob Roy - This is a favourite of mine, also known as a Scotch Manhattan, which is basically a James Bond style vodka/martini, where you use whisky instead of vodka. It is simply 2 parts peaty whisky, 1 part vermouth, a dash of angostura bitters, and finished with a maraschino cherry. Try it with a peaty whisky such as *Laphroaig*, it is amazing.

Rusty Nail – 1 part whisky, 1 part *Drambuie*, served over ice with a lemon twist garnish. Simple.

---

[32] www.theguardian.com/global/2010/sep/12/nigel-slater-classic-cranachan-recipe-whisky-oatmeal, www.bbc.co.uk/food/recipes/cranachan_66101
[33] www.scotchwhiskyexperience.co.uk/scotch-whisky/whisky-cocktails.php , www.whiskymag.com/cocktails/

Hebridean Sunset – a nice long summer drink. 2 parts whisky, 2 parts Grand Marnier, 1 part Cointreau. Shake with ice, top up with orange juice, add a dash of grenadine and an orange twist.

The Scotch Whisky Association also publish a few cocktail and food recipes you might like to try.[34]

The real deal

Once people are ready to try malt whisky neat or watered, it is probably best to start with a Speyside sherry casked whisky, then Lowland, Highland, Island, and finally a peaty Islay. The tastes generally move from light and sweet to robust and pungent. My recommended learners run would be *Glenlivet*, *Glenkinchie*, *Glenmorangie*, *Highland Park*, and *Laphroaig*, all readily available and reasonably priced as 10 or 12 year olds. After that, you are spoilt for choice. Use the guide to holding a whisky tasting and whisky tasting sheet in the appendix to help you get started.

"The best thing for a case of nerves is a case of Scotch."

---

[34] www.scotch-whisky.org.uk/understanding-scotch/enjoying-scotch-whisky/

8 WHAT NEXT FOR WHISKY?

Market trends show that Scotch whisky overall is not doing as well since its peak in 2012. In 2015 the Scotch Whisky Association reported[35] that the value of exports in 2014 dropped by 7% to almost 3.95bn GBP (6.1bn USD), while the volume of shipments was down 3% on last year to 1.19 million bottles.

In 2013, Scotland exported 27 million litres of single malt whisky worth 820m GBP (1.26bn USD).[36] Single malt was 8% of all whisky exported by volume, and 19% by value. Sadly for me only 9% of bottled malt scotch whisky remains in the UK, with the rest going to France (17%), USA (17%), Spain (29%), Italy (3%), the Rest of Europe (22%), and the Rest of the World (29%). Scotland is having to increase its barley production to cope.[37]

---

[35] Annual Review 2014 www.scotch-whisky.org.uk/news-publications/publications/documents/annual-review-2014/#.VXYGos9Viko
[36] Statistical Report 2013 www.scotch-whisky.org.uk/news-publications/publications/documents/statisical-report-2013/#.VXYIKc9Viko
[37] www.fwi.co.uk/articles/19/10/2013/141528/barley-growers-crucial-to-scotch-whisky-success.htm

At the moment there is high confidence in the Scottish Malt whisky industry. New boutique distilleries are up and running, such as *Abhainn Dearg* on the Isle of Lewis, and *Kilchoman* on Islay. Projects at various stage of completion include *Kingsbarns*, Daftmill, *Barra, Gartbreck, Wolfburn, Falkirk, Huntly, Ardnamurchan, Glenrothes, Strathearn, Cambo, Isle of Harris, Torabhaig, Walkerburn, Jedburgh*, and the Shetland Distillery Company[38] announced within the past few years. Unsurprisingly, mothballed distilleries are also being re-opened to meet demand, including *Roseisle, Glenglassaugh, Glen Keith, Rosebank*, and *Annandale*. Diageo have also announced major expansion at *Clynelish*. With these developments considered together, we can expect to see some very collectable bottlings coming forward over the next few years. The only fly in the ointment at present is the liquidation of *Bladnoch*, Scotland's most southerly distillery, but expectedly this will be bought over.

There is also now serious completion from other countries. In the UK we have the relatively new *Penderyn* in Wales, and *St George's* in England. Outside the UK, there is huge interest in whiskies from Japan. Names such as *Yamazaki, Nikka*, and *Chichibu*. Even the Scotch Malt Whisky Association now bottle and sell Japanese whisky in response to the growing market. These bottles are commanding incredible prices previously only though realisable by Scotch. For example *Karuizawa 1964* changes hands for around 10k GBP (16.5k USD) a bottle, and even 1000 GBP (1650 USD) just for a miniature. It's raising a few eyebrows that people are willing to pay for whisky from Taiwan, with *Kavalan* bottles selling for around 150 GBP (250 USD). Indian whisky is also gaining favour, for old timer *Amrut* and the relative newcomer *Paul John* which you can now find in Selfridges. So we can expect to see a fair amount of competition and choice, which is good for

---

[38] www.shetnews.co.uk/news/7382-new-plans-for-a-shetland-whisky-distillery

investors of course, but still makes us Scots a little nervous as to how this will impact on our industry.

It is well known that stocks of old whiskies are running out, as I discussed in Chapter 5. As you might expect, distilleries without old stock are fighting back, trying to shift the focus away from age. There has been a recent run on 'Non-Age Statement' (NAS) releases, such as *Glenlivet Alpha*, *Balvenie Tun*, *Talisker Storm*, *Glenfiddich Cask Collection*, *Macallan 1824*, *Aberlour A'Bunadh* etc.

There are some concerns about the long term quality of such whiskies, as it seems almost inevitable that the malt blend will be cut with younger whiskies as companies look to increase their profits. However the proof of course is in the tasting, and there is still enough competition in the market to keep standards high. Surprisingly this approach seems to be having some success, with such bottles being sold for prices similar to those of older aged whiskies. And from a drinkers point of view it is not all bad news, as we won't have to wait so long for new tastes to hit the market.

Some people argue that this is a welcome bursting of the whisky bubble, but I would offer another opinion. As long as Scotch whisky is seen as a sophisticated prestige product, with the heritage and status of cognac or champagne, there will always be collectors, speculators, and a profit to be made where supply does not meet demand. There simply isn't enough rare whisky to feed the appetite of the rising superpowers of Asia, their nouveaux millionaires, and their populations aspiring to try the things we in the West take for granted.

So enjoy drinking the old ones, because they will soon be gone. And remember, you can't take it with you. But with a little bit of shrewd investing, you can look forward to having a damn good retirement party either paid for, or supplied with, the best whiskies in the world.

Slainte!

"My favourite whisky? My next one of course!"

9 HOW TO HOLD A WHISKY TASTING

My first advice here would be to go to a tasting. And then a few more. You will soon see how it is done, and suddenly realise how it is that drinking a few whiskies can take a few hours. The fun of the process is not only in drinking, but having a good argument with the others in the room about what flavours you can pick up, and which whiskies are the best. There is no right answer of course, as everyone has different tastes, but usually there is some agreement that will allow a ranking.

Step 1 – choose a theme. Good themes to get you started are:
- The 5 (or 6) regions;
- One distillery, different ages e.g. new spirit,12, 21, 30 year olds;
- One distillery, different finishes – e.g. natural versus wine casked, rum casked;
- Grain versus malt;
- Round the world – whiskies from a range of different countries;
- Blind – where the whiskies are secret.

Step 2 - buy:
- 5 different bottles (using your theme);
- 5 Glencairn nosing glasses per taster, a special type of glass, shaped like a tulip, for whisky tasting. Ardbeg usefully sell one with a lid. If you don't have these glasses then it really does not matter. Use a brandy glass. If you don't want to buy so many glasses, just rinse out and dry inbetween;
- 1 Beer mat per glass, to cover up the whisky until time to taste, letting the smell develop;
- mineral water, for diluting, and cleansing your palate.

Step 3 - line up the whiskies in glasses, ordering them from:
- lightest to heaviest (usually peatiest);
- youngest to oldest;
- cheapest to most expensive; or
- worst to best (if you know/can predict this - both Jim Murray and Serge Valentine use a points system which you can use to help- just Google).

Step 4 – start tasting

For each person tasting, print out 5 copies of the whisky tasting note sheet provided at the end of this book to take notes on each whisky, Then it's time to get started.

1. Pour – 25-35ml is normal. You can use less if the whisky is expensive, you don't have much, or you think a lot will be wasted;
2. Colour – note the colour - you will need to get familiar with shades of yellow and brown;
3. Body – swirl in the glass and note the viscosity. More viscous and oily whiskies leave 'legs' which take time to fall back into the liquid;
4. Nose – smell the whisky. Sniff gently initially, as you may feel your nose burn;

5. Taste – take a sip and swirl around your mouth. Also feel the texture;
6. Water - add a few drops, or a small dash (5ml) if you found it too strong neat. If you are worried about adding too much water to the whisky in your glass, try the reverse. Take a swig of water, a sip of whisky, then swirl together in your mouth;
7. Nose - as before;
8. Taste - as before.

For those of you that want to do your tasting alone in the peace of your own home, there are quite a few companies that cater for that with miniatures, such as:

- The Whisky Tasting Company (who also supply The Times Whisky Club). Their packs are readily available without buying a membership e.g. on Amazon, Virgin Wines, etc;
- The Whisky Tasting Club;
- Master of Malt 'Drinks by the Dram';
- The University of the Highlands and Islands Moray College/ Gordon & MacPhail Whisky Course;
- The Wright Wine Company Whisky Sample Club;
- The Whisky Shop San Francisco;
- www.whiskysite.nl.

Some companies offer good mixed packs of their own whiskies, such as *The Classic Malts Collections*, or *Macleod's Regions Minipack*. Or you can just buy a range of different miniatures e.g. using Ebay (other than Ebay UK), or whiskyauction.com, which has two specific sections for miniatures only.

If you want to go to an event organized by others, good regular tastings are run by the Scotch Malt Whisky Society (varies outlets worldwide), Nickolls and Perks, Milroy's of Soho and a number of festival listed in Chapter

5.

This past few years I have been lucky enough to go to tastings by Balvenie, the highlight being tasting a very dry old whisky from my birthday year 1971, Glenmorangie, to help choose their next release, now named as *Companta*, and several by the Scotch Malt Whisky Society, being on my doorstep. These are a great way to build your knowledge and meet like-minded whisky lovers that might just have the bottle you are looking for, or want to buy that rare one you have.

"What whisky will not cure, there is no cure for"

10 WHISKY TASTING NOTE SHEET[39]

Distillery	Expression/name	Bottler
Age	Distilled date	Bottled date
Strength % vol	Bottle no.	Maturation casks
Date of tasting		

---

[39] Other tasting sheets at pribblebabble.wordpress.com/tag/black-dog/page/2/, www.whiskyfun.com/SergeTastingSheetV3.pdf , www.awardrobeofwhisky.com/content/files/whisky-tasting-paper.pdf www.whiskymag.com/nosing_course/part1.php ; Other tasting systems at gluttonyboys.files.wordpress.com/2009/12/tasting-sheet-rev1-51.pdf, whiskyscience.blogspot.co.uk/2011/07/flavour-wheels.html, , www.whiskymag.com/media/nosing_course/Whiskywheel-Big.jpg, ,

	Neat	**With water**
Colour		
Nose		
Body		
Taste		
Finish		
Opinion		

Taste Prompts

CEREAL
Cooked mash - cooked maize mash, tun draff, cooked potato skins, hens' mash, Weetabix, porridge, bran, cattle cake
Cooked vegetables – cooked swede boiled, corn, baked potato skins, sweetcorn, mashed potato
Malt extract - malted milk, Horlicks, Marmite
Husky - chaff-like, dried hops, mousey, pot ale, iron tonic
Yeasty – meaty, gralloch, Gravy, pork sausages, boiled pork, roast meat

ESTERY
Citric - oranges, tangerines, mandarins, limey, peel zest, Kiwi fruit, nectarines, pineapple cubes
Fresh fruity - banana, pear drops, green apples, lemonade, peaches, apricots, greengages, fresh figs, cherries, gooseberries, Victoria plums, raspberries, fruit salad, ripe pears, strawberries, fruit pulp
Cooked fruit - stewed apples, stewed rhubarb, candied fruits, fruit in syrup, wine gums, fruit gums, rum-toft, marmalade, raspberry jam, boiled sweets, banana rum, rotten fruit
Dried fruit - raisins, sultanas, prunes, dried apricots, dried figs, mixed peel, christmas cake, mince pies, black bun, Dundee cake, prunes
Solvent - paint thinners, nail varnish remover, ethyl alcohol, barber's shop, brylcreem, turpentine, bubble gum, American cream soda, artificial fruit sweet, cigarettes, acid drops, fresh paint, pine essence, cellophane, saccharine

FLORAL
Fragrant - perfumed, scented, rose, carnation, coconut, coconut milk, gorse bushes, chrysanthemum, lavender, wild flowers, lilac, honeysuckle, air freshener, fabric softener, Chanel No.5, scented soap
Green-house - geraniums, green tomatoes, violets, flowering currant, florist's shop, Parma violets, tomato leaves, sherbet, Love-hearts, apple, mint, spearmint, peppermint
Leafy - green leaves, lawn cuttings, crushed green bracken, green sticks, cut grass, laurel leaves, green vegetables, pea pods, sappy fir trees, pine cones, pine nuts
Hay-like - dry hay, coumarin, herbal, mown hay, heather, flowers, barns, hamster cage, sage and onion, mulch

PEATY
Medicinal – TCP, iodine, sea-tangle, sea-spray, carbolic, coal tar, soap, neoprene, germoline, Friar's balsam, Benylin, Ether, Victory V's, surgical spirits, hospitals, diesel oil, lint, bandages, tar, creosote, menthol
Smoky - guaiacol, burnt wood, bonfires, wood-smoke, scorched paper, peat-reek, smouldering embers, exotic smoke, burning cinnamon sticks, Lapsang suchong tea, incense
Kipper - smoked salmon, smoked oysters, smoked mussels, anchovies, dried crab shells, dried shellfish, sea shells
Mossy - birchy, earthy, fresh peat, turf, moss, water sphagnum moss, bog myrtle, fishing nets, hemp, ropes

FEINTY
Honey - mead, heather honey, flower honey, pouring honey, beeswax
Leathery - new cowhide, digestive biscuits, mealy, poultry-food, leather upholstery, calf, book-binding, libraries
Tobacco - fresh tobacco, stale tobacco-ash, rolling tobacco, aromatic tobacco, tea chests, tea pots
Sweaty - furniture polish, piggery, stale yeast, lactic, cheesy, buttermilk, baby vomit, sickly, old gym-shoes, dirty laundry
Plastic - scorched plastic, plastic buckets, oilskins, plastic macs

SULPHUR
Vegetative - marsh gas, drains, bogs, brackish, stagnant, spent matches, turnips, cabbage water
Coal-gas - exhaust fumes, brimstone, minerals matchbox striker, cordite, spent fireworks, dirty shot-gun barrels, hydrogen sulphide, acetylene, calcium carbide
Rubbery - new rubber (tyres), burnt rubber, pencil eraser, Bakelite, industrial, electric cables
Sandy - elemental sulphur, hot sand, sandy beach, linen, fresh laundry, starch

WOODY
New wood - sap-like, resinous, pine-like, cedar-wood, cigar boxes, sandalwood, sawdust, orange peel, ginger, tannic, spicy, peppery, cloves, allspice, cinnamon, nutmeg, curry powder
Old wood - musty, fusty, cork bung, cloth, blotting paper, cardboard, newspaper, mushrooms, damp cellars, mould, old books, earthy, metallic, inky, tinny, wet iron, pencil-lead, chewed pencils, paraffin, naptha/camphor
Vanilla - glycerine, custard powder, treacle toffee, butterscotch, fudge, caramel, tablet, Russian toffee, sticky toffee pudding, caramel wafers, toffee apples, creme caramel, golden syrup, brown sugar, meringues, treacle, condensed milk, barley sugar
Toasted - burnt toast, roasted malt, cocoa, coffee, rice pudding skin, brown toast, burnt cake, coffee grounds, aniseed, liquorice

WINEY
Sherried - oloroso sherry, fino sherry, sauternes, chardonnay, madeira port, burgundy, brandy, drinks cabinet wine, vinegar
Vinous extractives - brown sauce
Nutty - marzipan, benzaldehyde, walnuts, hazel nuts, Brazil nuts, almonds, praline, roasted peanuts, rape seed oil, gun oil (Youngs 303), linseed oil, sun-tan oil, mutton fat, tallow, candlewax, oiled wood, olive
Chocolate - milk chocolate, bitter chocolate, butter cream

"Friendships are like whisky - the older the better."

ABOUT THE AUTHOR

Dr. Michael J. Ross is a Scottish author. His books are intended not just to entertain, but to educate.

Michael holds the Whisky Course Certificate of the University of the Highlands and Islands Moray College/ Gordon & MacPhail, and is a member of the Scotch Malt Whisky Society.

Having obtained a doctorate in chemistry at Strathclyde University, Michael worked at universities in the USA and Australia before coming home to a change in career and completing an MBA at Napier University. He currently lives, works, and writes in Edinburgh with his wife Anna, who also enjoys a dram or two.

Michael can be contacted at rosswhisky@gmail.co.uk.

Printed in Great Britain
by Amazon